D1598920

Harpo Marx at Prayer

OTHER BOOKS BY SAUL BENNETT

New Fields and Other Stones/On a Child's Death
Jesus Matinees and Other Poems (Chapbook)

Harpo Marx at Prayer

Poems

Saul Bennett

Archer Books

Certain of these poems have been published previously by *Peregrine, The Christian Century, Icarus 97, Will Work For Peace (Anthology)*, babysteps.com, RecursiveAngel.com, *Hodge Podge Poetry* and *New Fields and Other Stones/On a Child's Death*.

Published in the United States by:
Archer Books
P. O. Box 1254
Santa Maria, CA 93456

First edition

Library of Congress Cataloging-in-Publication Data

Bennett, Saul
   Harpo Marx at prayer / Saul Bennett. -- 1st. ed.
    p. cm.
   ISBN0-9662299-6-7 (pbk.)
    I. Title

PS3552.E547543 H37
811'.54--dc21   00-056590

Printed in USA

E-mail: harpomarx@archer-books.com
Web site: http://www.archer-books.com

For All My Dead and Those Near

Contents

III

Supplication

Alone

Past eleven or twelve I longed to play
"Alone" on the harp.

               (I longed to play Alone
          I longed to play alone
     I longed to play
I longed)

If as a kid you were loco over the Marx Brothers,
and wasn't I, till Sara's death, when I quit the fool
for so much I used to love, you too love "Alone,"
  so luscious,
    in tango time,

and already, I see, I open on me
the scrapbook of a High Aspirant
who manages only scraps,

as not only do I not pluck "Alone,"
I cannot, could not, will not, ever.

For a fact, let my rap-sheet show
I never so much as laid
a running tag on a harp.

If you are coming up short but remain
sufficiently spiritual to wish
to learn more,

"Alone" is that recurring gush
of a love song drenching the madcap
of "A Night at the Opera," the Marxer
revived soon after the War;

his giggly prankster pop eyes hammered
flush for once, so sits banker-earnest
Harpo, stowaway stroking solo before adoring
beauties surrounding his instrument
down in that soundstage steerage
...so luscious,
    in tango time;

I, rocking along with them,
    alone (as it were),

gorging, one dime-thin wheel at a time,
half a pound in all, peeled off waxy deli wrap,
on kosher hard salami spread across the bottom
of a November Sunday afternoon inside the late
Loew's Woodside (site today of St. Something's R.C.)
bunkered beneath El cars racketing a-clack *still picking*
their noses along our cramped Blue Coal corridor
of butt-end Queens where you were born how
or learned by six to make your fists go a-pow! *against*
late afternoons ringing bells in the Hib four-storeys
pushing your Please Help Palestine! pushke *into pinked,*
grumpy civil servant pusses dreaming, no less b'Jeez!,
of splattering a Blatz in your fat little Hebrew face.

None did. Over the years a few startled,
with a nickel. Once, a saint disguised
as a fireman fed my box a quarter,
    so luscious,
        in tango time. . . .

16

I

Sinister Submarines Savage 'Sitting-Duck' Shipping Warranting Wilson's Warning Words, War Weaponry Building Boom, Boosting Allies' Fighting Fortunes

WHILE REITERATING NEUTRALITY, PRESIDENT ASSERTS
U.S. WILL ACCELERATE MUNITIONS PRODUCTION,
SELL ARMAMENTS TO GREAT BRITAIN, FRANCE

I.

There go my father's brothers,
seventeen and sixteen that suspenseful summer,
taught tall tales by strangers, fingers
bay-windowed across shady lips,
of the mounds of jack awaiting big boys
building bombs a universe away.

In the spirit of their mission
they're dressed to kill — *oy!*
Observe *tsvai boitshikels* in lumpy-kneed
knickers softly crowning slack sox,
billed caps serving platter surface size,
fleeing with Pop's permission his post-Pale

New World lodgings atop his tailor shop
hard below Flushing choo-choo station;
first, aboard a pre-Columbian
Baltimore & Ohio rail coach caught
at the Jersey City ferry shed;
later, flashing weathered, fixed-bayonet

thumbs, hitching in horn-honk
waltz time over the top By Jupiter!
cutting through the Huns' wire at Venus!
standing fast the gas of Mercury!
landing, *farmischt*, at last, on the Nitro,
West Virginia bomb palace constellation.

II.

Returning home men, *nu?*, a year later
for kid brother's bar-mitzvah in '17,
my uncles haul so-so stash
of cash for the family but
glorious piles—don't ask!—
of filigreed tapestry

tales, strung high, of high explosive
Nitro nights.

For his age, tall, my father, thirteen,
said Sabbath's star, sighs regrets to sis, nine,
Nitro's glycerin nights
had not claimed him too.

My Father Shot In Philadelphia

My father shot in Philadelphia
at twenty-five
targets him alone inside a dark
close-fitting overcoat before
a local monument missing
a hat against snow.

His retiring smile
and her message on the back suggest
another
fancying him years before Mother.

In Transit Lies Life Everlasting

Waving make-believe good-bye to him
  at three

Wedged between his sister
  and my mother

I turn ahead but turn again
  to see

My father from the middle
  distance smother

Fear of never seeing
  him again

With a broad arc of a wave
  that smiles

Me on our way aboard in
  light rain

On the World's Fair tractor
  train for miles

A Tattooed Man Awaits His Execution

My grandmother's porcelain egg cups appeared
wrong for the Bronx
walkup in the heart
of the heart of what today some see
as terrifying "Fort Apache."

Egg cups to a boy looked lordly,
grand receptacles, made maybe for
Roosevelt, reigning then, or God
help the Jews if he got in, some said,
Dewey. Dainty, they were, brought over,

I wonder, from a shtetl? Wiggly violet lines
embracing the faintest remains of
daffodil adorned their ivory skin,
corseting the soft boiled shells within.
Hunkering into a cup an egg was a tiny
tattooed man shaved bald before electrocution.

For Cassia Berman

The Hungry Aftermath
of Marxist Dogma

I once watched Chico Marx as close to me
　as an eye chart peel a banana
　　on the Roxy stage in his swing band
　　act between movie showings.
Though feeling Chico less funny
　than Harpo or Groucho and missing
　　Zeppo in their later pictures
　　I couldn't get over being brought
Way down front from Queens
　with eats after by my mother's
　　first cousin Belle and her half-a-head-
　　shorter stogie husband George
Who'd bought War Bonds enough
　for free tickets. As their 1-A
　　son Sheldon turning eighteen
　　had just been called up
Wanting a kid that day I suppose
　they took me. Chico so close was so old
　　between "A Day at the Races"
　　and "A Night in Casablanca"
And even at eight I thought his routine
　too dopey. Audience laughter barely tied
　　coughing or maybe I was too
　　fidgety to hear straight inside

My eats daydream thinking where
they'd take me after hoping for
the Automat at least and maybe
the audience was hungry too.
Heading out after Cousin Belle asked
hadn't I loved Chico and there were
little George's stogied lips
twitching hard for an answer.
To disappoint might mean
not no eats but maybe less
or less good. So he was funny
all right I said and all
That bought was a frank
and an orange crush at a Nedick's
subway stand standing up.
Thumbshooting stray
Relish droppings off that streaky counter
the way I shot marbles fifty years ago
I learned tell the truth
and food will find a way.

Nags

A small-time gambler who drove for bread
 a mob front waiters' coat and apron laundry
  service truck, my first floor friend Bernard's
   father Milt once came around wearing a white
    bakery string for a brown shoelace.

Inside that pocked oxblood moccasin I imagined
 convening tarted-up Greenpoint Avenue
  store window charlotte russes and kibitzing
   poppy-seed *hamentashen* as late winter Purim neared.
    I must have been eleven.

Years before Milt had coaxed my folks
 to their first and only trip to the track, probably old
  Jamaica, where he offered to bet for her
   my mother's dumb luck pick-by-cute-name
    long shot in a late race before vanishing.

When my mother's flesh crossed first, a giant
 apology, Milt reappeared. He told her they'd shut
  the two-balloon window as he'd hit and shot my mother
   back her deuce. Though my father's nature
    was forgiving, when Milt's name came up

thereafter, my mother alleged he'd pocketed
 her pot. Yet she never was less than cordial times
  Milt whooshed into our apartment to collect
   Bernard, radio adventuring with me, for their ritual
    divorce agreement Astoria early-movie-and-milkshake

Friday evening out. Sometimes he even took me.
As we had no car I depended. Milt's cars were never
  the same. Once he drove us to a Decoration Day
    doubleheader in an eaten-out DeSoto coupe
      with my father up front and a wooden milk bottle

crate for Bernard and me to split for a back seat.
  When Milt saw the sellout he slipped
    a Polo Grounds scalper two-and-a-quarter apiece,
      a tough half-a-buck over face, and treated us all
        to right field lower grandstand reserved.

The night of the bakery string I overheard Milt
  telling my father four grand it'd cost for a couple of
    Maspeth precinct detectives to lose his prints
      in a hot appliances fence. Nutty, his fingers there,
        Milt swore before my father.

As with the other grownups visiting that evening,
  my mother offered Milt in one of her cheery
    flowers-growing-up-the-sides cheese spread
      glasses a nice belt of Hoffman ginger ale
        but failed to engage him.

I wondered later if she'd spotted Milt's
  bakery string and, with me, assumed
    he'd tripped over tough times
      and felt sorry, maybe, a little.
        Bet a deuce she did.

Confectionery

A man missing a leg sat whole
afternoons after the War at our corner

candy store fountain drawing tiny beads
of Coca-Cola through that wide-hips
green glass bottle, smoking throughout,

crutches slumped beside
the next stool, speaking to no one

save Blanche,
the widowed proprietress's
youngish spinster daughter.

The two stared at every customer,
eyeing with premium suspicion
us kids,

and when an adult left, with a Camel,
or a "Late Races" *Journal-American,*
or a Blanche-dipped pint
of Meadow Gold Butter Rum, one
or the other might speak no more

than four
or five
words.

In those moments, floating
behind her wet confectioncry,
arms pressed across a faded print
flattish chest,

Blanche was waiting,
you supposed, for him
to propose.

"Delicatessen,"
As Rendered By Brueghel The Younger

In local kosher delis men at supper sat at
   long tables wearing hats,
strangers often plunked together forking sour
   green tomatoes, half-sour
pickles bobbing in a common briny wooden pool,
awaiting boiled brisket platters, mushroom-barley soup
poured at table by laconic waiters
from dented tin service cups into
   worn porcelain bowls.

Most hardly bothered to converse. Women were
dotted throughout but thinly, the tableau maker's
afterthought, and some, too, wore hats, little ones,
troubling rarely to talk with husbands or other men
who brought them (not to suggest, please,
for the love of a *kishka* plate or a corned-beef-on-club
smeared with Russian, a favors exchange).

Against this feeble glow of quiet a mysterious din
akin to the force of Flushing El cars flowing overhead
came often to overtake the arena and, once,
when an ancient waiter lost a load of dishes
I heard a patron's laugh like a firecracker   *Hah!*

On The Menu At The Asia Food Shoppe, Sunnyside, Queens, 1949

Sounding more sophisticated at mid-century
than chow mein to my mother, subgum became
the minor rage Sundays at Chinese restaurants
situated along the El line in our canton of Queens.

Ordering, in a raised voice, subgum in an eat-out
—you wished to be overheard, of course—
was meant to say, after the War, you were stepping
out smartly in an age when "smartness"

stood for *suave*, polish, no little derring-do
—picture an early chopper lifting you, say,
from the roof of the RKO Corona, dropping you
at the outskirts (you remembered your camera!)

of some loftier culture. And where is subgum today?
No one I see has seen it in years, *years.* I recommend
you question closely— grill it—chow mein, although
by now, I would imagine, chow mein, after interring,

summarily, its upstart rival subgum, in bitter decline
for ages itself, has died somewhere in Queens,
long known, owing to, a surprise to many,
its number of cemeteries, as the "Borough of the Dead."

Rocks

From their back room they sold you
if they knew you
and you called ahead
to this one family Auto Supply
gefilte fish they worked up themselves
in big pots on a stove behind a curtain
like Prohibition.

My mother
for the holidays would go there around
the corner across under the El from Sunnyside Garden
where my father took me to the fights
fifty for the winner a watch to the loser.

Their recipe was so delicious
the mothers said
big carp
and pike boulders spiked
with carrot pebbles shuddering
in a pond of pale yellow jelly
they sold on the sly smelling
against front-of-the-store
new rubber and sunny precious
oils enough to grease
every Polo Grounds seat.

When mothers asked for it they winked
but never gave away
their recipe.

Sicilian Indians Attack Homesteaders In West;
They Burn, Loot Large Settlement;
Many Said To Perish;
President Cleveland Leads Mourning

First, cuts off their heads, granting bodies
    breathing room;
next, jackknifes into quarters, roughly,
    their remains;
then, burns these crooked, black
    cigar parts for fuel
in his museum-rickety, hooked stemmed,
    like Sherlock Holmes's, pipe,
my friend Angelo's Sicilian mother's
    never-speaking-English father;

our dour ancient's custom surgery a blistered
bench protruding from the peeling shingled waist
of his next door "P A R K$5 MothlYOnly"
    watchman's job hut;
every-day-outdoors face over-bronzed a nearly
    car lot bottom coal
and a good twice as veiny as his hacked cigars'
    wrapper leaf;

his blazing bowl an ocean vessel's stinking stack
    slanting aft,
making forty knots easy in friendly breezes,
simmering stump signaling subtle kisses toward
    serenading sister ships.

But behind that rising blue accordion of smoke,
green olive eyes, oil fired wily-wet, begin to twist
    the old man's tale.
Statue rigid when he stands, tilting some to starboard
    in that posture hoary age adopts,
our seasoned skipper slips, suddenly, into a cunning
    cigar store Indian
chieftain's spectacular headdress, celebrating,
    in crematory silence,
sacking of the paleface settlement his warriors
—*Why, only jes' days ago,*
    the telegraph office is tellin'!—torch!

1951, After Smetana's String Quartet No. 1 In E Minor ("From My Life")

I.

Cubans smoke brown
   wearing waist up
      only old fashioned
         shoulder strap
            white cotton ribbed
               undershirts below
                  the El at 14th
roll in track slatted shade at store front window benches
undercreamed coffee color filler into khaki wrapper leaf
they bring to close with Island tongues and unguents.

Outside, McCarthy terrifies. At his end, in the Bronx,
DiMaggio aches. Round, still, are many
   television screens.

A dime, in sum, supports this daily habit: one quick
twist at the nickle neck of a subway Spanish
peanuts globe; Winchell bleating on the Reds
on Page 10 in his *Mirror*; an early *News* to track
the Belmont nags; a chocolate twilight
egg cream at a fanless stand awaiting morning
   tabloids.

Or, scan this: two nickels dropped in metered verse
liberating Union Square Automat burnt baked beans
crowned with underdone bacon inch in hat-size
   faux-earth crocks.

Truman pots MacArthur. Papa stews as critics steam
Across the River and Into the Trees.

Or, plunge your pocket hole burning Mercury
dime into a single grand, rolled-by-hand,
   beneath-the-El, Perfecto.

34

II.

                              No Cuban
so long as I look down looks up although
their lips behind their inmates' glass
suggest a little gab. Some nurse through gauzy
straws a Mission Grape or Pineapple.

                              Shvitzing
overhead halted June El cars gold-brick,
toweling dry against the splintery boardwalk
platform edge, winking with relief at homebound boys,
with softened fists, is all they need, to tease bully
    pulpit era wooden doors from closing.

                              Up there
in that fragrant Fagin air, Stuyvesant High School
boys who can't resist, those to be: Nobel Prize
in Physics 1990 nominees, celebrated Scarsdale
plastic surgeons, downtown Brooklyn
mob front lawyers, fall back, above the track,
to milk for free, against the law, penny Hershey
chocolate slots, raising Flatiron high index sores
    by morning.

                              Soon,
Buddy's Soft Custard stand, hard
by the Cubans, raises flag proclaiming
FREE! Dime Cones To Stuyvesant Boys
and Irving Girls With 90 (Proof!!!) Report Cards.

                              A Cuban
rolling in his leaves looks up,
spots sign, smiles,
shrugs, rolls.

Even In Warmest Weather The Woman Who Always Wore Long Sleeves

All that walks of Holocaust
Survivors now themselves
Deceased, Shulamith Marx bears on

A faintly spotted apricot
Cheek a not displeasing cinnamon
Mole, exhibits caramel

Hair in a bun
With the softest roll.
Privately,

She teaches violin.
Though smaller than those
In my dreams her breasts

Are not so small at all
And her warrior's strut,
Thrusting forth, lets them almost

Canopy me
Alongside Mother next to
Shoe Marks on our street.

Maybe Miss Marx someday will take you
As her student. And later alone with me
In the camps she already

Was Grown.
God knows
What went on with her.

Admission To The Academy

I was shown into a great room showered
by sunlight so immense
in an upper loft
on lower Fifth Avenue
and stood on a stage or
broad platform before
the father of my apartment house
next door friend Paulie
and for the next fifteen or twenty minutes sized
as my father watched.

So deliberate was Mr. Schnitzer's
touch, fingers
threading about but never poking, or
his tape, even
in the slightest, restraining, but *conducting*,
this maestro of measurements! As I was
fat, the calling out by Mr. Schnitzer
of my numbers to his assistant
embarrassed, but as only
sixteen and with a lifetime to lose
weight, I remained awed,
not discouraged, and just
a week later, materialized
if not by Mr. Schnitzer's own
fine hand, fashioned to his diligent
if slightly imprecise specifications, the navy

serge suit itched me up to a seat in the rear
of the balcony of the Academy
of Music near Union Square for graduation.

Raising One With Jesus In Chicago

For twenty hours each year before Christmas,
Before the aeroplane arrived at America's
Business standard, a railroad car contained

My father to Chicago.
His company's only Jew and observant,
He made the best of these home office

Jesus birthday *soirees*. Though a spirited
Salesman my father never volunteered
To take a drink. But in Chicago

He more or less had to—this was their way.
Not, mind you, he appeared
To mind. He enjoyed his two

Or three rye-and-gingers
Each year and an old
Chicago photo has him smiling.

A Chocolate Lunch

She had me, my mother, one lunch,
take my father in for a suit.

An earnest dresser whose cuffs routinely
swamped his shoes, he bowed to her
request. After the fitting he thanked me

for choosing a milk chocolate number,
as in that age a man
brown to business in New York was
not mocked behind his back.

When he died a year later
we gave away the suit
or buried him in it. Either way
it remains delicious.

Quarters

Before my eyes my father
  died in three
    -fourths of an hour. "I hurt,"
      from my bedroom doorway
he said. "I cut
  an orange for you."
    Then he lay down.
      I believe now
forty years after he was in
  pajamas. We were alone,
    my mother in the hospital having a
      breast cut off.
I made for the kitchen and polished
  off a quarter. The rest
    of that orange today
      still smells. I called
the doctor. A long time
  he knew my father. He got
    over in half an hour, my father
      rolling in their bed con-
vulsing. He gave him
  a needle or two.
    Then the doctor—
      it was August, you see—

made it to the droning room
air conditioner and back to us
began to cry against that almighty
hum. Some odor. In a gold
and black silk
rep necktie I was taken
to the hospital. "Daddy
died"—and threw myself
over her. *I want to live!*
she screamed past
and through me clinging
to the headboard bars.
Owing to her slow
to heal chest they wouldn't
let her to his funeral. Anyway,
she died a year later.

Glass

For a living my father sold
surgical glass for a major operation
in the belly of America
that as a practical matter

excluded Jews. Because he came
a young man with a tiny Jewish
firm annexed in 1936
my father was granted

a stay. He stayed a salesman
but rose up, in a way,
to sales executive, bossing,
including himself,

a Rockefeller skyscraper
two-person office. "Eastern
Branch Manager," his card said.
As his father had instructed him to hit

the road for work halfway
through high school, a Jew forever
short a secondary diploma,
my father remained approximately

frozen. I'm not sure he minded
that much but it burned
my mother now and then.
He was productive and respected

by customers for his adored
test tubes, beakers and slides. For him
the affection of some seemed
love, it came out when five days before

scheduled semi-retirement suddenly
he died. Condolences appeared from many
in the organization. In the deep cream
stationary of one, a *bona fide*

sales executive who began
with my father, an eternity
past postmark, still, you can bathe,
generously, in the brokered tears.

To the widow was typewritten
he was sorry he, who could have done
more to advance her husband,
should have and had not.

Prosthesis

Now in November
after Father's summer
sudden death, in his memory,
Mother, weak, wishes
to push off
painting the apartment at
the lease's birthday but
the landlord says decide:

Now
or three years.

Spied against
her bedroom's invigorating
white bouquet, abandoned
for the night, squatting,
plump, on a dresser top,
a giant pointy-headed
pin cushion, or midget
bolster.

Next morning,
rising early, having slept on it,
you see it is
a breast she had removed.

Balance

My mother I can recall
sitting up in bed balancing

a checkbook ten days before
death, in conversation

the first time in weeks,
her last, appearing unaware

or unfazed the cancer could kill.
Gauging her chat that Halloween

nearly forty years ago I believed in God.
Toting numbers our freshly minted

widow expressed plans: a move
at last, still, to a larger apartment,

Thanksgiving, and so forth.
The nurse shrugged when asked after

if the thing had turned around.
"Better ask doctor." God not

withstanding, afraid, I could not.

A Citizen Recalls
A Country Outing In Wartime

My mother's *Rosebud*
was *cherry pail*, composed
on hospital room terminal

patient afterlife
lips hardly more
than half the age of

Kane's; like him,
out cold sighing warm
secrets, almost her life

awaiting release
to the more congenial
custody of her

kid recircling self.
As she tagged *Murray*,
her elder brother's name,

to *cherry pail*, I made
a picture, stooped over
her bed, pleading, I suppose,

the main trunk of me, to die
with her, of the two
on a rare—call it

exotic, for first
generation American big
city children—Great War

summer day country
outing picking cherries,
might as well shot

to the moon from home
in Harlem, Jewish then
on many streets.

Decades ago
my mother was heard
to whisper it.

Since, even
lean cherries
are plump.

Funeral Destructions

Her husband, instead,
I was said
to be,
on the tiny marquee

They stood outside the chapel.

And though I forbid,
asked the night before,
lifting of her lid,
for mourners to straw more
of her clear
to the bottom; entering, early, from the rear,
I spied,
emerging, periscope-wise,

Her nose, a powdered divine
cheek, above the coffin line.

When I shouted, or wailed,
their uniform crew, with precision care, sailed
down to batten Mother.

"Easter Eve In Washington Square," After The 1926 Aquatint By John Sloan

"When you begin a poem," my sister asks,
"do you see it all before you?"

After a pause, "I see it sometimes
from inside a taxi."

I

I'm a Nineteen-Thirties cabby
dipped in fluid midtown traffic
intense and if alone upfront
unlonely at my wheel

Though my passenger is silent seated
dignified behind me we are one

In a gown-length black spring coat
pinched slender at the waist
—not to say unattractively severely!—
beneath halfmoonish gray-pearl cloche

she appears at three or four my mother

II

We slant south toward lowest Fifth
where Sloan drew her at sixteen

—my invention at first sighting of
his drawing not long past her early death—

between two other noir-lit starlets hugging
overflowing cones of flowers underneath
umbrellas past the Arch at Easter Eve

III

Embraced by teeming sidewalks fleeting
anecdotes float toward us forming
strangers who respond with earnest waves
though softer than their slashes
formed to flag our cab

Others in the street appear
to wish to start a conversation
recalling with some passion
unremembered leavings from her past

I speed a little noticing a universal grin

IV

As the crowds begin to break
rote details fill in her story's space
like pink and easy attic insulation

On the weathered leather jotter
of my mind my notes of her
are dense and fleshy on the flanks
but spare if tender at the center

For Susan Mishler

Walking Wall

I used to walk Wall Street nights.
Pine. Beaver. Cedar. Stone. Curl
up Pearl. Stalk the Slips. Campaign
Maiden Lane. Searching, alone, old
New Amsterdam for my kindred
beginning almost forty years ago with no job
and false prospects, looking to the dawn
of New York to glide my spirit home.

Discharged of life except for random pins
of window light, the towers dripped
on intravenous. On Front the dozing giant
coffee roasters elevated scent. West off Rector
Trinity's coffins rolled. The Automat on
Church, so sad to say, was dead till dawn. Dead, just,

my father, mother—once he took me to a steamship
office down there somewhere
near the Battery where a man he knew
heaped into my hand with a huge
"Some lucky boy!" freighter passage to Antwerp.
Then they were dead. Which was why I walked,

I suppose, to find them there, somewhere
south of Spring. I spoke to no one through
the night. Panhandlers, the few, I ignored. I adored
the old original subway stops, august terra cotta
plaques on platform walls pronouncing
each station's Edenic origin. I favored Bowling Green
for its cuddling half-moon ceiling. Very late from there

the subway rolled me home to Queens.
Crusading north in empty cars past Brooklyn Bridge
I watched for Worth Street station. Gone,
you see; you saw its tawny ghost. They'd closed it
when my parents lived. There — *there*,
they were, at some time, in some form. Or,
at station City Hall, abandoned after I was born.

They are down here
somewhere. I should search some more.

Death's
Dotted line
Is a door
Ajar
Eternally

Overheard on the subway

The Dismantling Of An American

I stopped with all the American
business after my child died

suddenly; the Brooks-bloop
button-downs, their pants without

pleats, flags on holidays, baseball
cock-a-doodle-doo with clients, age eight

bourbon, Bean catalogs, crab
claws. I was this—Jew.

II

Harpo Marx At Prayer

Starting, say, six, a boy brought to watch worship,

I came soon to see, seated, smiling, facing
*   west, with all the rest,*

an old boy, or a young man
*   —with that hat who knew?—*
who could not speak (an old man whispered to my father).

He came topped that morning and always
in all seasons across the years by a wintry camel
broad flat cap with five sharp twinkle-star points
and a long bill in the old style—

a throwback boy/man like Daddy's uncle
in his picture on the boat to America.
His eyes were tinted grownups' after-services
apricot schnapps and jiggled like the steel
balls shot off by my pocket pinball toy

whenever the doors of the Ark teased open.
With such eyes and no speech he was
that silly man with the funny brothers
in the movies except the other kept on
a black high hat. He came only with his mother,
this poor mute, no taller than she,

and she was short, for a mother even,
and stooped, over her head hanging a black
kerchief folded flat, like a mat; stout,
with strange, faint skin between
white and orange, painted a melting
creamsicle pop like the pictures
of old ladies in the two-subways-away museum.

Though, again, she was stout, this was only
with her eyes open. Davening, *shut,*
she appeared to shrink; swaying
south, north, back, rocking in silent devotion time,
eyes hiding small secrets, getting themselves ready
to go someplace good, after, maybe, with him,
after the schnapps. All my life, God could tell you
why, I've adored them, their Jewish romance.

Nineteen Hundred

Imagine a hundred years ago
your mother's grandfather, lost
in Spanish though five years there,
entreating authorities in the Argentine
to allow his Tsar-hounded lot

entry to America?

Who spoke? Grandma, conversant but eighteen?
Big sister Tante? Brother Yankel? Wily, gentile
friend? Had their pleas been feeble would today I be
another aging Entre Rios tango star? Reappeared
ghost of a *Desaparecidos* Jew "Disappeared?"

Never Mind The Jews

Never mind the Jews
last century lent the universe
Freud, Einstein, the Marx boys
to cut through things a different way.
More pointed is how they came
to cut sandwiches in the New World.
In their narrow ghetto delis they built mounds
of meat so high, dense, stuffing brisket, rolled
beef, boiled tongue, various smoked flesh
inside bursting seeded rye walls,
who could hold and eat at once
even half of such an edifice?
So ahh . . . the Jews devised sandwiches in
thirds, slicing first across and clean through the neck,
slashing top to bottom in half the remains,
a regular Cossack pogrom hacked etiquette.
Who says we don't emulate our oppressors?

Survivors

I *Transport to the East, 1942*

I.

Did you ever see her
after? Did any body?

Last observed late autumn encamped
in dying rain, at musty dusk,
on a high honking outpost snuggling
Bloomingdale's,
when the doddering El, dusting down Third,
still brushed that emporium's bosom.

Not slender; middling fair; hair:
snooded, auburn, generous;
at thirty-three, struck back against noir-washed
59th Street subway kiosk bars in this
rationed Checker war year—ahh! there! the one
fondling at her collar fox in a muted blues
plaid woolen blanket, an infant;
gripping, dropping, gripping
digits of a boy perhaps six,
assigning him on release custody
of his sister, freeing mother to hit
the gutter *to Heil! Again! Again! Again!*
20¢-drop/5¢-each-additional-1/4-mile cabs?

II.

As it happens,
she merely was bringing them a new
way home, only half, this once, by subway,
from a day with her Bronx parents,
but as the boy framed forever
those moments, ignored in inglorious
teeming; sighing, so, mother; unhushable,
keening sister; no father (off on
an overnight business trip);
fleeing the echo of morning
radio word of another *Wehrmacht*
penetration deeper into Mother
Russia, who could say these three
Jews could survive,
subsequently, transport to the east, if
only across the river to Queens, if
a taxi never were to stop?

II *Mush, 1943*

So worn
by Nineteen
Hundred
Forty-three
the husband
of the sister
of my mother's
mother

lay in the Bronx
in bed all day
forcing up
to greet the soft
and hot tan
cereal

Tante parachuted
to him from
a cruising spoon

His yarmulke
was square
and flat
a perfect plot
a cake

of black
that fell
and rose
and fell
as slow
and agonized
as smoke

each time
his pillows
pushed him
toward the gruel

It came out after
Simcha died
that even
as his mush
went down
fresh pits in Poland

near from where
he came

were swallowing
warm relatives

III *A Jewish Child is Poured Cocoa, 1944*

In the War, say in '44, when I was seven or eight,
   I told my mother
after school one day I was going to play over
   that Saturday at William Zellner's,
a boy in my class, to trade stamps with him. Please,
   she said, don't go,

And she told me the Zellners were German,
   from there, his mother and father.
I understood, in a way, and when he came home
   from work my father
took my mother's side. Finally, anyway, I went.
   William's mother

And his father, even, were so nice. They gave us plenty
   of attention and smiled
and joked, or seemed to, more than other parents,
   maybe because, who knows,
I was this Jew. As William and I swapped stamps
   on the rug

In their living room, William's mother brought us
   piping cocoa, then refills.
I had stamps in my skinny collection from Germany
   with Hitler's head on them.
Or maybe Austria. My parents didn't know.
   I can't recall swapping

Any of them with William but maybe I did. When it all
   came out after, I wondered
what William's parents' relatives were doing then,
   and how, and where, where especially,
and what William's mother and father would have done
   at a different address.

IV *Let's Pretend, 1945*

Owing strictly to geography
a Holocaust escapee, concurrent
with incineration over there
of girls and boys my age,

de rigueur pasting over here
by roaming neighborhood
Irish bar-mitzvah
age thugs. My incarceration boundaries:

west and north, Harlem's
Polo Grounds' upper deck
overhang in right; dropping south,
to Rockefeller Center Saturday morning

"Let's Pretend" live audience
radio studio; swinging east,
over water, to Queens,
our block, my mother, sickened

by shanty housewives' *Jew!* barbs
blow-gunned down on her
from corner walkup snipers' windows,
finally skipping their sidewalk,

clinging, instead, to the gutter.
If you count this last routine
a horrid beating, if a pounding,
merely, on the heart,

and add for pocket change
my *Fat little Jewboy!*
random dustups
surrounding, say, early '45,

Frank's date, and I today abhor
but fancy guilt for still remaining,
is it just too patronizing
to claim *Survivor!* too?

Shut

                                        Firing spittle
the kid's rubber mouthpiece popped
when on his belly he landed in
black trunks inside two minutes,
round one, thud smacking of a great steamer
trunk *guillotining* shut, a startling
clumpf! He just lay there, you know, eyes flung
shut, canvas absorbing a raspberry balloon
cheek for a cheap watch (half a yard to the winner)
around our corner at the old Sunnyside Garden
where my father took me, Tuesday treat,
truer to life, he said, than wrestling Wednesdays.

Before me, not all that long after
Hitler, and though Italian
on the program his name appeared, as he was dark,
dark, pummeled, the kid today is another specimen
Jew stripped to shorts, camp summoned,
surrounding, to witness his martyrdom,
                                        swinging.

"Hitler" Preaches On Wall Street, Mobbed By Jews; Goebbels Active Near Trinity Church; No Arrests

An early postwar American
fascist, Kraus—tattooed name!—
went at it afternoons at Wall & Nassau, just a short
trail of imagined swastika flags distant
from the Stock Exchange.

"Little Hitler's" sermons routinely grew
a tight circle of beefing Jews; young,
silent, not altogether unsympathetic, you saw through
their opaque smiles, Irish back-office clerks,
the random high-rung

Darien snap-brim Member Firm White-Shoe,
and straying 75c-an-hour after-school
messengers like me. At fifteen,
though Kraus as a rule

inflamed alone, I hated less
than feared him. Pounding before
rabid clippings stabbed into beaten easel boards
he implied annihilation. Behind him
the pursued in me saw

forming up toward Trinity's spire the midgety
Goebbels, uniformed, solitary below a bursting
 *Seig Heil*ing!
grandstand, waving a ceremonial first
torch over a pyre of defiled

Torahs. Why hadn't the Jews crushed Kraus,
wrecked his stand? I asked one, an old
hand with a beard. "In America, this is different."
Occasionally one rode past, but you never saw
 a patrol car roll

Kraus up. I know, all right, I know—*free speech.*
Anyhow, the louder the Jews honked back,
the softer swanned Kraus, parched smile unyielding,
gouged, today, out of that mustachioed avenger in Iraq.

At Bottom

In this town near the bottom of Ohio
you were made in the Fifties
to thumb forty miles toward the top
to the nearest qualifying city

for a professional haircut by the hand
of your own kind were you
a rare, and to the bottom's
barbers, exotic, campus

Negro, barber explaining to me lashed
to his chair, *Theirs's wool ain't hair*
tops exceeded his scissors'
jurisdiction and charity, before

lumbering off on a long, circling
but dead steady walk over Jews.
Dropped there at sixteen by
assimilationist parachute

I regret to tomorrow
I said nothing, even going back,
he scalloped gentile
bottom vogue flattops so beautifully.

For Diane Sears-Bugeja

With The Atomic Spies
At Rockaway Beach, Queens,
June 1953

When the bark springing from
their little radio condemned again
and finally Julius and Ethel

to death, in the flaming sand
a blanket away
the Irish *hoooed!*

"Atta *way!* Six-three to croak them
Jew spies. Leave 'em fry, hah Kevin?"
"You got it, Mac—burn 'em both, hah girls?"

Flesh slathered, bellies down,
the dates could only moan.

Page One, next morning, a partial
box score of this sporting event:

*Ethel Rosenberg, the 37-year-old wife, entered
the death chamber a few minutes after
the body of her husband had been removed.
Her hair was close cropped on top to permit
contact of an electrode.*

"Mrs. Rosenberg sat in the electric chair with
the most composed look you ever saw,"
one witness said.

The first of three successive
shocks was applied at 8:10 1/2 p.m.
After the third shock the two
doctors applied their stethoscope and found
she was still alive. After two more
applications of the current—but let it go.

I'm not taking sides understand
—just reporting events from the desert
on the festive eve of another Irish holiday.

Fearing

Fearing a Jew? Fearing—Kenneth Fearing,
the poet. You'd think so—see his photo
in this old anthology I hold. American, Fearing—
a novelist, too (b. 1902)—*The Big Clock*, later a
movie mystery —but skip his story.

You tell me: paunchy nose;
pretzel ears (broken too, you'd say, the nose);
dark, dark hair, crinkly—oh, a mountainous black
demi-lune; eyebrows, not aquiline. But black,
the look, the eyes; snap, probably shot
late Thirties, or in the War—regardless: Hitler time, shot
    (or worse).

Cut, his head, from my father's family's mold.
To begin, an elder brother. Survived
only as they were on this side,
you know. Ran out of the old
Pale, 1880-something, Grandpa, pogroms, orphan
boy. Yes, Fearing could be one of them.
Not that he was. Not that he was

this Jew, sliding—but he might be
    (hiding).

Washington Armory

Imagine a livelihood
selling inside those walls
Holocaust Museum memorial

candles? Running stalls
dishing little lamps
burned on memory's *Achtung!*,

or, instead, invading camps!
Liberating Zyklon showers
in your house of business; tiny death

repelling flame-throwers
melting high fences, gates,
when still life breathed inside?

When a friend states
he knows of a man in
Yartzeit candles there,

I do what I can
here to torch history in eighteen
lines. But I'm no angel.

For Howard Greene

Ovens

The sight of an old man

With a tattoo

Number

On his forearm

Entering the chamber

Concert shed

Blew open the mouth of the Christian

Sabbath

Summer

Oven

On The Death Of Hitler's Secretary

DUSSELDORF, Germany, July 16 — Fifty-two years after Hitler's death, a personal secretary to the Nazi dictator who remained with him until his last days in a Berlin bunker has died in a hospital here. Gerda Christian, who lived to 83, rarely spoke about her work with Hitler. "What am I supposed to say about that?" she once asked. "Whatever I say would certainly be misinterpreted."

Was Der Führer
 flatulent?

Did a typing error rate
 a pinched chin?

Did Frau Christian suspect Der Führer suspected
 a Jewish grandparent?

His breath—was it
 sickening?

Giving dictation, did he pick
 his nose?

Did Frau wish to show Der Führer a little
thigh? Did you plead, Dear God, to have Der Führer order
you to undress? Did you long to pound his
lips with yours? Were you, after all, in love? (Answer!)

Come, Frau, was Der Führer's farewell gift no more
 than a generous hug?

Pray, Frau?

III

Deceiving Jesus

*In the prime of the mute there appeared on our block
       a beggar*

*covered by a cap colored a filthy beet in the mushroom
form worn by Brother Chico, singing songs for
pennies and dimes mothers squeezed into kleenex*

*they wafted from windows in the tenements and better
       60-a-month apartments.*

*No pack on his back he was not even a low peddler but
a mere tramp preceded by a twisted stick, lacking all
save a little rosy guile and the sweetest
tenor, ancient and pure, peddling instead of a Yiddle's
       foghorn lament "Eyye . . . caashh . . . clo-ohs. . . ."*

*"Roses of Picardy," "Marta, Rambling Rose
of the Wildwood" after radio's Street Singer,
and with wily lungs for tenement cents, "My Wild
       Irish Rose."*

*Who but Hitler wouldn't pity such a lump: face
blistered, swollen, scorched with sores, red always
—so what if it was wine? as a mother tight
       with pennies charged.*

*Once, home from school sick, I threw down on him
my only quarter with five pennies, an early
       heaven down payment.*

*(I retain today a daydream of the shul mute crooning
through June screens the beggar's songs Sabbath
morning; after, the beggar, seated, smiling, facing
       west, with all the rest,*

thundering, like some Galitzianer *Thor ,*
a service-closing Ein Kelonheinu *before*
beating it back for the apricot schnapps,
L'Chaim!-*ing them at the herring-and-honey-cake*
  Kiddush table

then kissing, once, the old mother's cheek before
  a smiling Harpo. . . .)

One summer Sunday Freddy the block bully slammed
pennies to our sidewalk but pointed the sound to a steep
landing behind a high fence. "There! A lady threw
money there!" The sweating beggar it took an age
to scale then jump to find nothing. Frightened Freddy
would pound me good if I spoke I said nothing.
When the beggar climbed back Freddy repeated,
  then again.

In his young thirties Freddy picked up
cancer and died. God, all right, had taken him for
deceiving Jesus, sparing me fifty years to die inside
  my first child's death at twenty-four.

Drunk Forever

Horrific grief
inebriates
touching off a forever
bender
stinking up the heart's
breath till time's
beginning
rotting stockpiled rations
of hope
buried since birth inside
our cells
appearing bearded
baldish
balmed by burning
tire incense
rat-tat-tatting without
end with the crook
of its gnarled staff
against your brain
flailing
Now you have a taste
little man—drink!

The End

In the months that pummeled after
he came to feel before he saw them
those who came to see him next might
save him. Awaiting them he told

what trailed before him in the mirror
They will say something
in a way to make this mostly
go away. So they came

and talked, and sat, and talked, for hours,
patting his knuckles, lipping his cheek, hugging
loosely in the end. But when they went
it stayed, his child's sudden death.

His, Then The Nun's Tale

When she came courting the nun
no taller than a lawn jockey
offered a knob of a hand and shook
mine and though looks plain
her immense smile spoke through the sunlight
between our fingers, hers plucking mine,
great chords and persistent.
When she released mine I felt her fingers
sense they could have anything
they wished from the booty of my tribe.

Half again as tall as I
this man stooped to me
and when I brought
my hand to his he seemed
 Lord knew why at first
his eyes
  to chant.
"Sister," he began," I am of another
 faith."

And then his eyes'
 agony dissolved.

He said his child had died and though
I am only of a cultural order our eyes'
height then I would say was the same
 and we embraced.

However

Usually the eyes fold first. No longer
water resistant, they burn just
a touch before searing your insides
out. Composure is important. The wet
can be arrested if you will only stretch to their
limit your eyes, taking spectacular breaths.

However, lacerations pierce your throat,
a terrific stale burn renewed.
At the same time, a certain trailing
soreness sets inside your right eye (if you are
left-handed, as am I; I can't speak if
the reverse is so). A vague press
upon your stomach could follow.

However, the right eye remains
your main concern, though over time
(half a minute perhaps) that fire passes,
as do you, into what passes
for a present, after another
unplanned visit to the alabaster bank
of memory of your dead child.

.

Little Guy

Meet a midget of mercy
masquerading as a kind
of angel of same.

Inform me you found
this morning your mother
dead in bed after a pause

hear my "O—my—God. . . ." but note
no exclamation.

Or, your wife ran off
Or, your child flunked out
Or, your husband won't admit
you into his premier thoughts
Or, even—even—your child's

limb needs cutting off;
yes, my wings
I shall make appear to
enfold you but these are a paper
bird's and raw against gossamer.
Steel, they were; steel, you bastards!
before my child's sudden death.

Shopping

Around the third year following her death
in her twenties you find your child

has advanced from offspring to colleague
and peer. As she no longer has a life

discussions center less on events personal,
more on those worldly. Imagine, as for example,

strolling behind a cart you roll
together with her in a supermarket aisle,

going on about your problems at work,
confiding your delinquency again on life

insurance payments, questioning France's
motives in Iran—all right, extreme.

Oddly, then, a child dead drifts, over time, into
a spouse. Odder, you find yourself

expressing her response to your view
on such topics to her mother, who stares.

Guilt Edge

As parents we all have our limitations.
You couldn't make enough
for private college tuition.
You? Youngest still in rehab? *I?*
Unable merely to prevent my

child's death. You fool, you oaf,
you might counter—no *doctor* could.
She was dead instantly.
Aneurysms, my boy, are
not cancer. I know,

but so? What's a father
for if not to rescue
his child? That she dropped,
brain, *poof!*, like that, two hundred
miles from where I sat talking

up a client, is, as the French
fascist Le Pen characterizes
the Holocaust, a detail of history.
Jesus, in time I'll be taking on Holocaust
water: I let that one sink too.

Below

I was struck today by the clutch
of poems inhabiting basements:

shopping for our child's
coffin in the funeral parlor

underground; retreating
to our basement at home, alone,

to scream, evenings, once
the drug of early mourning wore off;

ascending, at last, from beneath
to the curb, carting for garbage

our mourners' hard box seats,
treasure hidden there a year and a month

past *shiva*; journeying down after
delaying two years to exhume

for Cerebral Palsy her cartoned clothes.
Perhaps below poems mean

to stress to me I live today
as a practical matter there.

Flight Number Whatever

Over the air a woman
whose child went down
in an unsolved terrorist fashioned crash
was saying *No!*—she was not

a better person for her pain.
Worse!—angry, envious, small, ruined.
"Where," she bawled, "is justice?"
Father of a child, twenty-four, dead,

naturally, I felt relief,
as another, at least, whom I never
would catch and perhaps hope
to mutilate had not murdered mine.

Move

Emptying, at last, her dresser drawer I fell
   across a tidy swarm

Of ticket stubs—Mets, Knicks, St. John's, Triple A
   ball on vacations,

Rock, the odd horse show. Late Eighties, early Nineties.
   Adrift alone

In that bog a '96 clasped my eye, cheering me,
   for, after all, dead,

She had, dropped, at twenty-four, in '94. Or,
   for that eternity,

Had she? Or, thought had clasped. Swear.
   Honestly.

Dating Game, 1998

Say, as mine,
your child died in 1994.
You open the paper to the movies
on TV today, hoping for a really

old one — say, from the Thirties,
but suppose you settle
quickly for a '54? Now, carefully
deduct this differential

of 44 from 1998
and add the sum to your daughter's
twenty-four, her death age,
for a projected life of 68 years,

approaching Biblical span—not half
bad. But now you guess
that had you waited
till tomorrow,

a '42 might have
been yours, thus granting her another
dozen years. With fresh
guilt you grieve for shortening her life.

Nothing

In the shack we share
in the woods near the house
my daughter and I convene.

She died four years ago
almost, suddenly, twenty-four, leaving us,
younger brother, sister. Our children came
less than two years apart.

We moved, my wife and I,
last year, left the density.
The children are in the city.
I do a little consulting
from the house and make
poems in the shack behind.

A good number of the poems are about her,
us, sometimes the five of us.
God doesn't tap my shoulder.

The place has nothing in it,
nothing: stone floor,
cracked;
raw walls;
eaten away foot
wide plank ledge—my desk. I stand.

Moving newspaper soft black copy pencils
without erasers from my old days
I compose, revive in fine point fountain pen
green, harvest,
ditch, reluctantly, overripe
darlings, dreaming
out the unwashed shallow window
that won't open.

Around,
the place mustn't be much
more than six feet. There
we converse in her element. There I feel nothing
comes between us.
Nothing.

I'm Beginning Again

I'm beginning again to inhabit the life
of my child as she lived; within,

to begin, the particular puff
of her cheek; entering that puff

and the drowse of her breath
without a token now, dissolving into

the subway rumble of
her laughter, regularity of her gait;

modeling the embodiment
of her voice, becoming her

conversation, most particularly
with me, on her return, her elbow

poised on the doorway
jamb of her room I thought

to sit in
to grieve.

Delay

In the head you hold before you
exhibits alleging life—lofty pine, the withering
wire fence about your jungled garden, the odd
mailbox spiking the vacant rural road—sky.
But if these you sense existed when your
child lived, let them prove it real *today*. Delay, delay. . . .

Fourth-And-Long

A closing supper with my daughter drove the dream
the night before
another birthday
of her sudden death.

In a festive banquet setting blending laughter
with much milling
I stood behind her chair
near the axis of the dais
bending low to give a kiss.
With a playful shove she shooed me off rejoining
conversation
with her first and only
Love she'd kissed *Goodbye!*
off to work an hour
this side her end.

While I appeared to be departing
on a business trip
my farewell was interrupted by a stunning
Roar from within
an adjacent domed stadium into
which I'd wandered
alone.

I had come upon a college
football opener
pitting Roman Villanova against a certain
Virginia State A & M Normal
which though owing to that name I reasoned
historically Black contained
On the field caucasians only. Underdog
it quickly took then held
a shaky lead. Though isolated
On an empty grandstand end zone sideline
I felt the winning team's
twelfth man.

I wondered waking whether
I was trying thusly to be told
a miracle on a larger plain would fetch
my daughter back
when I returned. Or had I gone
While she remains?

The Child Who Comes To Visit

As if waked from mad sleep in the strange embrace
   of a beige straitjacket
   easing ever so;

above faded paint
   NO EXIT above gated
   hooded door at the foot of the ward;

scarlet neon oozing
on
   off
on
FIFTH YEAR SURVIVORS ONLY
WAREHOUSED ON THIS FLOOR;

flanked abed by crooning coo
   of a snore old man
   and awake jabbering drool of a fool

even older,
   his wet ignored by chunky stump
   of she-nurse patrolling

who halts at you, and smiles,
   and bends, and whispers, white cap
   points in your face suddenly

Satan's ears: "If you are cogent today,
   repeat, but mind, no
   screaming, *'My child is dead'"*

Selkirk Safe At Home

All returning souls came to count the same.
Clients, their wives even, from twenty years before,
and the woman who spoke her poem to him
    the night before,
and the eighth grade fill-in French teacher whose daring
unsupported nipples hung like summer
    inside her lilac satin blouse,
and from before his birth a shadow of the man his mother
said had sold her shoes then stole
    a pound in change,
and LaGuardia, Houdini, popes, George Selkirk,
    who succeeded Ruth in right—
each more luminous than the last refugee retreating
on those risen floats leaked beside his dozing wife
at dawn through bloodshot blinds by the encroaching
anniversary—sixth? ninth? fourth? whuh?—
    of his child's end.

Art

With a hidden finger I draw sometimes
across my trouser pocket lining

the number of my daughter, who died. Perhaps
one day I'll call, or she might.

Benediction

Listen Carefully

*I never listened carefully. Somehow I could
not. This seemed my nature
or fate. So I taught my expression to paint*

*earnest attention and thus brushed the top
of my field with compensation in a year
topping my father's lifetime pot*

*in our best years. As these yielded
slowly then swiftly to the ordinary then less
slowly then swiftly it appeared to colleagues*

*my paint ran. Others stood in for me
at times then almost always. I still hold
my title but important assignments*

*elude me. My staff is gone.
When you visit my immense office with
private bathroom I try to remember*

*to paint. I make my day go.
For my next birthday I have asked
our grown living children to bring*

*a workbook with pictures
they use in the second grade to teach
cursive script. I mean to start over.*

About the Author

Saul Bennett worked as a newspaper reporter, then entered the business world, which occupied him for many years, culminating in his appointment as president of a Madison Avenue public relations group. He is author of a poetry chapbook, *Jesus Matinees and Other Poems* (Pudding House Publications) and the poetry collection *New Fields and Other Stones/On a Child's Death* (Archer Books). Bennett and his wife, Joan, live in the Hudson River Valley in New York State.